Original title:
The Fruit Basket of Life

Copyright © 2025 Creative Arts Management OÜ
All rights reserved.

Author: Atticus Thornton
ISBN HARDBACK: 978-1-80586-305-2
ISBN PAPERBACK: 978-1-80586-777-7

Harvesting Hope

In the garden where dreams do sprout,
Lemons laugh and grapes shout out.
Pick the berries, wear a smile,
Life's sweet moments, just for a while.

Cherries giggle, ripe and red,
Waking joy from where we tread.
Plant the seeds of silly schemes,
Water them with bubbling dreams.

Nectar of New Beginnings

Peaches blush and pears sway right,
Welcome dawn with fruity delight.
Squeeze the juice from daily grind,
Life's a cocktail, well-defined.

Citrus zest, a cheerful blend,
Life's tangy start will not offend.
Shake the tree, let laughter flow,
New beginnings, watch them grow.

Tart Tales and Sugary Songs

Berry bards sing silly tunes,
Plucking fruit beneath the moons.
Tart and sweet in harmony,
Life's a feast of jubilee!

Glimpse a fruit with quirky grin,
Every bite's where fun begins.
Pie in hand, devil-may-care,
Slicing worries, sprinkle air!

Ripe Realities

Bananas slip, with joyous flair,
Reality's a dance, beware!
Grapes in clusters make a fuss,
Ripe adventures stir up trust.

Peeling back the daily grind,
Strawberry punch of every kind.
Tartness brings the laughs anew,
Life's a smoothie, join the crew!

The Orchard's Secret

In a grove where apples giggle,
Oranges dance with a little wiggle.
Bananas slip with a chuckle bright,
Pears gossip 'til the fall of night.

Peaches prance with a rosy glow,
Plums make jokes, oh what a show!
Cherries laugh in a huddled pack,
While grapes toss seeds to start a snack.

Fruitful Companions

Mangoes wear hats made of leaves,
While lemons share their bitter thieves.
Kiwis tell tales with fuzzy flair,
As pineapples joke in sun-kissed air.

Berries form a band so sweet,
Raspberry and blackberry have a beat.
They dance around in playful cheer,
Giggling loudly for all to hear.

Taste Bud Tales

Every flavor spins a yarn,
Kiwi strums on a fruit guitar.
Lemon sings a zesty song,
While watermelon hums along.

Papayas share secrets bold and bright,
As strawberries sparkle in the light.
Grapefruits wear glasses, smart and round,
Turning all the heads around.

Lush Lullabies

In the night, the fruits grow wise,
Peaches dream beneath starry skies.
Cherries whisper soft and sweet,
While melons sway to a gentle beat.

Bananas boast of their golden hue,
Kiwi tells tales of morning dew.
All join in a sleepy tune,
Swaying softly by the light of the moon.

Plucking Purpose

In the orchard of dreams, I climb with glee,
Hoping to find some ripe fruit for me.
One plucked too soon, it just rolls away,
Maybe I'll try a banana today!

Apples and oranges throw a big mess,
Chasing each other, what a fun guess!
Caught a peach that gave me a start,
Turns out, it's just a very round heart.

Tending the Grove

Pruning my worries, they grow like weeds,
Watering laughter, that's all that it needs.
Each tree is a tale that's waiting to sprout,
But watch out for squirrels—they're not here to clout!

Sunshine and shadows play hide and seek,
A cherry tree giggles, it's feeling quite cheek.
I dance with the branches, they sway with delight,
Bugs join the rhythm, oh what a sight!

Savoring Solitude

In a comfy hammock, I swing with ease,
A bowl of berries, I eat while I tease.
Each berry a secret, a burst of fun,
Sipping on juices while watching the sun.

Minding my own, I spot a bad joke,
A cantaloupe rolling—a sneaky little poke.
I laugh to myself, the world's quite absurd,
Alone but not lonely, joy's always stirred!

A Bowl of Lessons

In a big ceramic bowl, life lessons stew,
Picked ripe from the tree, oh the flavors are new!
An orange says, "Peel off your doubt,"
While a melon's wise words bring the fun out!

Each slice tells a tale, sweet and quite tart,
Reminding us all to play our own part.
So munch on your growth, don't let it go bland,
Life's tastiest morsels are made by hand!

Seeds of Yesterday

In a garden where memories sprout,
Lettuce whispers secrets, no doubt.
Carrots gossip with a cheeky grin,
While radishes laugh, it's a win-win!

Old vines tangled in tales of the past,
Beans argue over who's the fastest.
With tomatoes blushing, stealing the show,
Nature's drama, it's a wild grow!

Aromas of Abundance

Scented dreams waft through the air,
Garlic and basil make quite the pair.
Onions shed tears, but it's all in fun,
Their fragrance lingers 'til the day's done.

Fruits causing a ruckus in a lively crew,
Bananas slipping, and strawberries too!
Juicy chuckles as they tumble and roll,
A fruity fiesta, that's the goal!

Blossoms of Change

Petals flutter in the breeze so wide,
Change is coming, let's enjoy the ride!
Sideways daisies with a twist in their stance,
Waving hello, they invite you to dance.

Sunflowers towering, with heads held high,
Try to compete? Oh me, oh my!
A garden of giggles, colors collide,
In blooms of laughter, we all take pride!

Tasting Trouble

A pickle jar promised a tangy delight,
But sourness hit like a comical fright.
Cucumbers chuckled, they knew the score,
"Who invited the trouble?" they cried with a roar!

Falling apples threw a dance-floor spree,
Careful now, keep an eye out for debris!
With every bite, giggles seem to erupt,
A comedy feast, who's getting plucked?

Fragrant Moments

In a garden of colors, a dance in the sun,
Grapes giggle softly, they've just begun.
Bananas wearing hats, all droopy and bright,
Claiming they're kings, in this fruity delight.

Lemons trade jokes, tart but so sweet,
While cherries pop pop, swinging to their beat.
Apples are laughing, they'd roll if they could,
Juggling all flavors, oh man, life is good!

Echoes of Eden

An orange holds court, its peel all aglow,
Sassy and juicy, it puts on a show.
Peaches play tag with a sly little pear,
While strawberries gossip without a care.

Mangoes are plotting a grand, fruity feast,
With kiwi in charge, the laughter increased.
They sip on cool nectar, so sweet to the taste,
Life's fruity follies, no moment to waste!

Overripe Memories

There once was a banana, a tad too mushy,
Claiming it's vintage, not old and gushy.
Avocados whisper behind leafy screens,
Sharing their secrets and living their dreams.

The cantaloupe chuckles, "I'm more than I seem!"
While a wandering berry joins in the dream.
Nostalgia's a fruit salad, sweet with a grin,
Each bite tells a tale of the shenanigans in!

Citrus Hues

Zesty and bright, little lemons declare,
"Life's a grand party, let's strip off despair!"
Limes spin around in a citrus ballet,
Giggling and twirling, come join the soirée!

Oranges are singing with skins so divine,
As grapefruits boast, "It's our time to shine!"
Juicy confessions from each fruity soul,
In this merry orchard, we're all on a roll!

Melon Illusions

In the fridge, a melon dreams,
Wearing pajamas, or so it seems.
It rolls like a king on a throne,
While snoring sweetly, all alone.

But wait! A berry tunes it down,
"Get up, you fool, or we may drown!"
With laughter loud, the grapes confer,
"Your royal dreams? Just a big blur!"

Sweet Surrender

An apple tried to charm the pear,
With cheesy lines, it filled the air.
"I'm crisp and fresh, a lovely sight!"
But pear just laughed, "Oh, take a bite!"

Bananas swung in, wearing shades,
"You both look silly in juice parades!"
They split their sides, in fruit-filled cheer,
While grapes just giggled, "Bring on the beer!"

The Grapevine Conversations

In clumps they chat, these sassy grapes,
About their plans, and silly shapes.
"I'm the star of every blend!"
While tossing shade, they laugh and bend.

A peach chimed in, with fuzzy flair,
"Let's squash this talk, I'm too debonair!"
But lemons rolled, with zest to spare,
"Let's make a scene, it's only fair!"

Orchard of Openness

In this orchard, secrets bloom,
With apples talking, spreading doom.
"Did you hear what the berries said?"
"No, but I'm all ears, it's time to spread!"

A fig popped in, with tales so grand,
"Life's a jam, let's take a stand!"
With laughter shared, and roots entwined,
These fruit folks thrive, completely aligned!

Sweetness in Shadows

In the orchard, I trip and fall,
A peach rolls over, laughs at it all.
The apples chuckle, hang on tight,
As I chase melons in pure delight.

Bananas slip with a giggle galore,
Citrus zings with a joke to explore.
Grapes are playing tag, oh what a scene,
While berries pull pranks like they're on a screen.

Lemons squeeze juice into my eye,
Oranges tease me as they roll by.
In the shade of a fruit-laden tree,
Life's a comedy, come watch with me.

Slicing Through Seasons

Chopping squash in a summer breeze,
Carrots dance with a flurry of ease.
Winter's broccoli, all frozen and bold,
Tells tales of warmth, in whispers of gold.

Spring brings radishes, tiny and bright,
They play hide and seek in morning light.
Zucchini's hiding, it thinks it's so sly,
While onions are crying, oh me, oh my!

The seasons mix like a salad tossed,
In this kitchen chaos, what's truly lost?
With each slice and dice, life's rhythm flows,
In this juicy drama, hilarity grows.

Juices of Journey

Squeezing lemons, oh what a task,
But laughter bubbles up, who could ask?
Pineapple sings in a blender's whirl,
As mangoes twirl like a dancing girl.

Banana slips into a smoothie spree,
Berry blends sing, 'Join the party, me!'
Coconuts crack jokes while juggling lime,
All mixing together in chaotic mime.

With each sip, our spirits soar high,
As papayas burst and the good vibes fly.
Life's a concoction, sweet and bright,
In the glasses we raise, the future looks right.

The Flavor of Tomorrow

An apple a day, so the wise folks say,
But I'd rather munch on this wild parley.
Pineapples beam with a radiant glow,
Wishing tomorrow will bring more to sow.

In the garden of dreams, we plant the seeds,
With laughter as fertilizer, joy is what feeds.
Cherries giggle as they ripen so round,
While blueberries tumble, making no sound.

Tomorrow's flavor is daring and bright,
With a hint of surprise and a dash of delight.
So let's savor today, with joy and cheer,
In this fruity future, let's raise a beer!

The Pomegranate Path

The seeds of joy burst forth, so bright,
Each bite a laugh, a pure delight.
With juice that stains your favorite shirt,
You hop around, half covered in dirt.

Stumbling down this red-stained road,
With every snack, your laughter flowed.
Too many seeds, you start to trip,
A pomegranate slip becomes your quip.

When life gives you fruit, dance like a clown,
Messy and sweet, don't wear a frown.
Take a tumble, have a giggle,
In this fruity world, just shake and wiggle.

Pears of Perspective

A pear once said, with juicy grin,
"Life's all about the shape you're in!"
Falling from trees with a plop and a thud,
A funny sight, a soft green dud.

From orchard high to picnic fair,
Rolling 'round, without a care.
Laughter echoes down the lane,
As all the pears join in the game.

Not all are perfect, some get a bruise,
But still they shine in warm light hues.
Share a chuckle, find a pair,
In this silly fruit affair!

Citrus Dreamscapes

In a land where lemons wear bright hats,
They prance and dance like playful cats.
Oranges giggle, bursting with cheer,
As zesty jokes fill the atmosphere.

Limes twist and turn, full of delight,
Squirting fresh puns that feel just right.
Each citrus slice a piece of fun,
Creating laughter for everyone!

A grapefruit sings, a sour refrain,
Tickling taste buds, easing the pain.
In this garden, playful and free,
Life gets zesty, just wait and see!

Dreaming in Saffron

Saffron dreams in a golden hue,
A spice so bold, it tickles too.
Mixing colors, a swirl of fate,
Making stews that giggle and grate.

Cooks in aprons start to dance,
Whirling about in a saffron trance.
Whisking up potions that shimmer and shake,
Every spoonful a laugh that they make.

In this kitchen, comedy brews,
With every pinch, the laughter renews.
So sprinkle some joy, let it ignite,
In saffron dreams, everything's bright!

Palette of Perspectives

A banana slips with a chuckle,
Lemons giggle, oh what a struggle!
Apples tumble, plop and roll,
In this chaos, we find our soul.

Cherries crack jokes in the breeze,
Peaches tease, saying "Taste with ease!"
Grapes form a bunch, sharing laughs,
In the market of life, joy's what it crafts.

Juicy Journeys

Watermelons wear funny hats,
Traveling with fencing bats!
On a road of zest and flair,
Every bite brings a laugh to share.

Pineapples dance, sway to the beat,
Mangoes unite with sticky feet.
In this caravan of fruity folks,
Life's a party filled with jokes!

Harvest of Whispers

Carrots whisper to the peas,
What's your secret? Just share, please!
Berry bushes giggle at night,
Under the moon's silly light.

Oranges chuckle, peeling away,
Finding joy in every fray.
When life gives you seeds to sow,
Plant a joke, watch laughter grow!

Orchard of Dreams

In orchards where laughter grows,
Ripe dreams hang like sweet prose.
The figs make puns, a comedy show,
While pears nod along, stealing the glow.

The nuts crack jokes, all in good fun,
With every giggle, we come undone.
In this land of whimsical beams,
We pick the fruit of our grand dreams!

Nectar's Embrace

In a world of sweet delight,
Curvy grapes take flight,
Peaches giggle in the sun,
Juicy jokes, oh what fun!

Cherries whisper silly dreams,
Limes plot mischievous schemes,
Berries bounce in merry dance,
In this feast, there's romance!

Mangoes throw their tangy cheers,
While figs share fruity fears,
All unite in laughter bright,
Sipping nectar, pure delight!

From the vine to every dish,
Life's a banquet, make a wish,
With every bite, a wink, a grin,
Join the joy and dive right in!

The Lure of Lemons

Lemons yell, 'We're tempting folks!'
Their zesty sourness sparks jokes,
Lemonade spills in a splash of fun,
   Twists and turns for everyone!

Citrus blushing in the sun,
They know how to have some fun,
Tart gags shared among the crew,
Sipping sunshine, bright and new!

In a world where flavor sings,
Lemons wear their tiny crowns,
   Giving life a little kick,
With zestful quirks and playful tricks!

Watch the tales that citrus weave,
In every slice, a laugh's conceived,
   Join the party, don't delay,
   Lemon fun is here to stay!

The Taste of Time

Bananas peel back layers wide,
In the laughter, we all confide,
Seasoned years are fruitcake sweet,
With memories, each heart will meet.

Oranges spin a funny yarn,
Their juicy tales are never far,
Time brews punch like no other,
Sipping joy, my sister and brother!

Pineapples wear their crowns so proud,
Making us laugh, oh so loud,
Each taste a tickle, every bite,
Time's a feast of pure delight!

Cherry blossoms in the breeze,
Remind us of the zest we seize,
With every flavor, we shall find,
Life's a banquet, truly kind!

Orchard Impressions

In orchards wide, the laughter grows,
Apples play peek-a-boo, who knows?
Plums chuckle as they roll and sway,
In the breeze, they dance and play!

Every branch a jester's stand,
Fruits united, hand in hand,
Grapefruits yodel at the sky,
While peaches giggle as they fly!

Here, the seeds of humor sow,
With every bite, the joy will flow,
Orange puns and pear-shaped pranks,
Cheers resound in fruity ranks!

In every orchard, laughter rings,
A symphony of fruity flings,
So join the fun, let spirits lift,
Life's a harvest, our greatest gift!

Harmony of the Horticulturist

In the garden, green and bright,
Tomatoes tango with delight.
Pumpkins roll with laughter loud,
While carrots dance beneath the cloud.

Spinach whispers silly jokes,
Cucumbers chuckle with the folks.
Eggplants wear their purple gowns,
While radishes pull funny frowns.

The corn stands tall to grab a laugh,
While apples plot a cheeky gaff.
Each veggie joins this merry crew,
In the plot where giggles grew.

Harvest time brings joy and cheer,
Bananas slip, and laughter's near.
In fruity fun, we all partake,
From tree to table, let's all shake!

Strawberry Serenades

Oh, strawberries in polka dots,
Singing sweet (and silly) thoughts.
They jiggle on their leafy perch,
While raspberries roll in a merry search.

Blueberries burst with big ol' grins,
Joking with the peaches' pins.
Juicy tales from every vine,
In this berry patch, we all dine.

Their laughter bounces on the breeze,
As cherries play beneath the trees.
Fruit-confetti fills the air,
In this sweet world, we've not a care.

When winter's chill comes creeping back,
We'll just dress in berries, bright and slack.
For in this patch, there's never rue,
Just fruity fun and laughter too!

Echoing Peach Melodies

Peaches sway in summer's song,
They giggle right where they belong.
With fuzzy coats and cheeks so round,
Their laughter echoes all around.

One said, "I'm not a grapefruit!"
"Nor a prune!" another fruitlet hoot.
Banana plays the silly fool,
While lemons squeeze, trying to ruling school.

In a peachy orchestra of fun,
The jam's not just for everyone.
They sing sweet tunes while shaking branches,
While chatting up the grape romances.

So if you hear a giggle near,
Join the symphony without fear.
For in this orchard, laughter roams,
Each fruit a note, we call it home!

Gathering Edges of Flavor

Let's gather round the flavor feast,
Where every bite's a wacky beast.
Lemon twists, with cheeky flair,
While limes jump up with zesty care.

The nectarines hold court and jest,
Claiming they're the very best.
While olives roll their little eyes,
As everyone drinks from fruity pies.

Pineapples wearing party hats,
Invite the cranberries and their chats.
A peach parade marches through the door,
While apricots shout, "We want more!"

Each subtle taste brings smiles wide,
No boring bites for us to bide.
In this gathering, spirits soar,
With each sweet flavor, who could ask for more?

Bountiful Harvest

In the garden, things get wild,
Tomatoes blush, they seem like a child.
Carrots hide, they play peek-a-boo,
Lettuce shouts, "Hey, I'm here too!"

Peppers dance in sunlit spots,
Cabbages wear their fancy pots.
Radishes sing, they're quite a show,
The rhubarb giggles, "Look at me glow!"

Zucchini's lying, claiming to be tall,
While beans are climbing up the wall.
The corn gets jealous, wishing to sway,
As pumpkins roll around and play.

A banana slips in with a joke to tell,
"Life's a peach! Oh, isn't it swell?"
With all this fun, who needs a fork?
Let's eat it raw! Pass the cork!

Orchard of Dreams

In an orchard filled with giggly trees,
Apples throw jokes like a playful breeze.
Pears take selfies, posing just right,
While cherries are planning a wild night.

Oranges wear hats, so whimsically bright,
Lemons roll by in a citrus delight.
Plums are debating who's sweetest of all,
While peaches get ready for a summer ball.

Grapes gossip under a leafy cover,
Talking about the juice they'll discover.
A coconut arrives, with a bashful grin,
"Shell we dance? Let the fun begin!"

This fruit fiesta, it's quite insane,
With every bite, there's laughter and gain.
So join the revelry, let's all partake,
After all, life's a slice of cake!

Ripened Reflections

In a bowl so bright, the colors clash,
Bananas peek out, all in a flash.
A grapefruit grumbles, "I'm sour, you know,"
While berries argue, putting on a show.

Figs are whispering clever little rhymes,
While fruits sit back, sharing their crimes.
'Who stole the berries?' they all shout in glee,
A mischievous apple, 'It wasn't me!'

Kiwis are juggling, skills on display,
Tangerines laughing, in a bright ballet.
Melons are rolling, they want to compete,
In this fruity game, there's so much to eat!

Come join the fun in this fruity space,
With every bite, we quicken the pace.
Life's just a party, so come and chew,
This bowl of joy is waiting for you!

Colorful Cornucopia

A basket filled with stories to share,
Grapes tell tales of a grand affair.
Peaches are dreaming, all soft and round,
While lemons bounce about, making a sound.

Apples swap secrets, crunchy and sweet,
Bananas are slipping, quick on their feet.
Tropical fruits are hula dancing,
In this colorful place, joy's advancing.

Cherries giggle about their red cheeks,
Watermelons roll, trying their tricks.
Kiwi cracks jokes, fuzzy and bright,
Creating a ruckus, pure delight!

Gather around, let's savor the fun,
Life's like a fruit salad when all's said and done.
So grab a spoon, dig in with glee,
This rainbow of flavors is waiting for thee!

Aroma of Autumn

The leaves fall down like apples from trees,
Squirrels gather them with hilarious ease.
Pumpkin spice lattes spill on the floor,
Laughter erupts, who could ask for more?

A walnut jokes, "I'm hard to crack!"
As berries giggle, saying, "We've got your back!"
The pumpkin yells, "I'm feeling so round!"
While the hayride gives giggles all around.

A corn maze twists like a funny dance,
Our lost friends wonder, "Did we even stand a chance?"
The cider flows, sweet and so neat,
As laughter's aroma makes life feel complete.

The Sweetest Words

Honey drips like poetry in the air,
With sugar-coated secrets that we all share.
Marshmallows giggle in their fluffy white coats,
While caramel whispers funny little jokes.

A kiwi dreams of being a star,
While limes roll around, thinking of far.
Cupcakes in tutus dance around the room,
As cherries tease, "Don't forget the perfume!"

Chocolate tells tales that make you chuckle,
While licorice twists, oh what a shuffle!
Each sugary word makes our hearts twirl,
In this world of sweetness, we joyfully swirl.

Pulped Memories

In a blender, memories whirl with delight,
Strawberries giggle, taking a flight.
Bananas split into laughs, you'll see,
While oranges peel back layers of glee.

A grape takes a tumble, rolls to the floor,
Says, "I'm just trying to settle the score!"
Pineapples declare, "We're folks of great zest!"
As smoothies toast to the very best fest.

Cherries pop up with a joyful surprise,
While limes sourly grumble, "We're wise!"
Each sip is a giggle, each gulp a delight,
In pulped memories, we laugh day and night.

Between Leaves and Lyrics

In a book of leaves, songs flutter about,
Each page is filled with a whimsical shout.
A stanza of apples, ripe and so bright,
Another of berries, a playful delight.

Between the lines, grapes share a tale,
While the figs boast of their epic scale.
The melody swings from tree to tree,
As laughter and lyrics live wild and free.

With every turn, a new verse appears,
Sing with the fruits, let go of your fears.
In the grove where giggles and rhymes combine,
Life blooms sweetly, a hilarious line.

Melodies of Maturity

In the garden of age, we stir,
Pies baking slow, with a faint whir.
Lemons on trees, oh what a sight,
Bickering fruits, they dance every night.

Bananas slip past the wisdom of old,
Cherries roll laughing, their stories retold.
Peaches forget their soft, squishy sheen,
While apples plot chaos, like they're in a scene.

Grapes gossip loudly, their skin full of charm,
Weariness fades, where all fruits disarm.
So here's to the laughter, the quirks we bring,
In the melodies of life, we all dance and sing.

Bountiful Journeys

Pack your bags, let's hit the grove,
With a rhubarb hat, we'll dance and rove.
Plums in the car, they plan a heist,
Taking the cherries, oh what a slice!

Oranges zest up every detour,
Mangoes' sweet whispers leave us wanting more.
On this bumpy ride, fruits roll and sway,
Laughing together, come what may.

Avocados debate who's ripe enough,
While berries argue, 'why can't we fluff?'
Yet through all the bumps and sticks we face,
Our journey's a banquet, a fruity embrace.

Nature's Color Palette

A brush in hand, let's paint the scene,
With vivid tones, and a sparkle, so keen.
Tomatoes blush while carrots play coy,
Cabbages chuckle, oh what a joy!

Pineapples wear crowns, some golden attire,
Raspberries giggle, their sweetness conspire.
The zest of life in each hue and shade,
As laughter and colors brush every glade.

What a palette, vibrant and full,
With comedic strokes, life's bountiful pull.
In this orchard of joy, we splash and we cheer,
With a shout of delight, let's paint while we're here!

Sweetness and Shadows

In a world of sugar, where shadows play,
The bitter and sweet have their own ballet.
Candy corn giggles, mocking the dark,
While licorice frowns, missing its spark.

Chocolate speaks softly, a smooth serenade,
Marshmallows drift, in a fluffy parade.
The sour ones pucker, in jest they unite,
For sweetness and shadows have their own light.

As jellybeans tumble, falling in heaps,
The laughter of fruits, oh it amply creeps.
Together they blend, in whimsical glee,
Creating a world that's delightfully free.

Nature's Farewell Party

The apples danced with glee,
While bananas played the tambourine.
They toasted with sweet berry juice,
As the watermelon made a scene.

The pears wore silly hats,
As grapes rolled on the floor.
With every laugh and silly act,
They lived to party more!

The oranges brought some zest,
But the lemons stole the show.
With citrus jokes and puns at best,
This bash was all aglow!

Nature waved a cheeky bye,
As all the fruits piled high.
With seeds of joy they'd spread around,
At this party, pure and spry!

Core Values

In a garden, ripe with cheer,
Where friendships grow like vines.
Tomatoes blushed, they had no fear,
As they chased cucumbers in lines.

The carrots told a joke or two,
But peas just rolled their eyes.
"Lettuce be friends!" they all cried out,
And pumpkins waved goodbyes.

Zucchini asked, "Who's on the dish?"
"Not me!" the beets would yell.
But all agreed, with a wink and swish,
"Together we'll cook up a spell!"

So in this patch of vibrant glee,
Their core beliefs rang true.
Unity with a side of glee,
In every fruity brew!

A Harvest of Heartbeats

With each pluck, there's a story spun,
Of laughter in the breeze.
A squash told tales of summer fun,
While cherries giggled with ease.

A disco dance from each ripe fig,
Made everyone join in.
Peaches twirled, they were so big,
They spun until they fell in!

Tomatoes blushed a rosy red,
As a carrot cracked a joke.
The corn suddenly lost its head,
From laughing, what a poke!

So here's to every juicy bite,
To the moments we hold near.
In this bundle, pure delight,
A harvest full of cheer!

Blossoms in the Breeze

The flowers giggled, did you hear?
As petals danced all day.
They whispered secrets, loud and clear,
In a colorful array.

The daisies wore their best attire,
While tulips played the flute.
"Come join our joyful wild choir,
We'll sing till night is brute!"

A rose said, "I'm the fairest, see?"
But violets rolled their eyes.
"We're all unique in harmony,
With fragrances that rise!"

So let the blossoms spread their cheer,
In colors bold and bright.
Together, fun is always here,
In nature's pure delight!

Pearly Moments

In a peachy world, we mush and squeeze,
Bananas slip away with the greatest of ease.
Mangoes giggle, they dance in delight,
While lemons crack jokes, oh what a sight!

Oranges roll by, all polished and bright,
They're like shiny marbles, oh what a fright!
With cherries in hats, they try to look grand,
But tripping on grapes, they just can't stand!

Apples take bets, who's the juiciest prize,
While plums tell tall tales, with youthful guise.
It's all fun and games in this sunny bazaar,
Until someone bites in, and here come the czar!

So here's to the laughter, the fruity parade,
In this zesty carnival, we've all got it made.
Keep rolling along with a smile on your face,
Life's just a feast, let's savor the taste!

Tidal Waves of Tart

A lemon in a swimsuit, ready to dive,
Splashing in a pool where the sour vibes thrive.
With cherries as lifeguards, guard duty is keen,
Watching all the antics in this zesty scene!

Grapefruit on floats, they bob and they weave,
While limes throw lollipops, "Who dares to leave?"
A pineapple DJ spins tunes of delight,
As berries start dancing under stars so bright!

Mangoes take selfies with a juicy goal,
While kiwi just giggles, "I'm on a roll!"
Tomatoes in chases, they squirt and they flee,
In this fruity ocean, hilarity's key!

So grab a plush orange, join this sweet play,
Ride the waves of laughter, come what may.
In this tangy escapade, we find pure fun,
With every fresh splash, our joy's never done!

Layers of Life's Cake

In the pantry of dreams, there's a cake piled high,
Frosted in laughter, with sprinkles that fly.
Chocolate layers boast of their fudge-dripping pride,
While fruit on the top just giggles, "We abide!"

The cherry on top, she's the queen of the scene,
Stealing the spotlight, if you know what I mean.
"Slice me up gently!" the cake whispers low,
"Or I'll start a rebellion, and put on a show!"

Strawberries chuckle, as they tease with a rhyme,
"Life's just like frosting, sweet, messy, sublime!"
With a dash of nutmeg, the spice of our lives,
Each crumb tells a story, where laughter derives!

So slice up that joy, and share it around,
With icing as laughter, let's spread it abound.
In the layers we find all the fun we can bake,
For life's just a party, that we all partake!

Slices of Serenity

In a world where bananas slip,
Grapes get squished with every trip.
A pear says, "Don't be such a bore!"
While apples bounce and shout for more.

Lemons laugh with zest for days,
Cherries giggle in fruity lays.
Oranges roll with joyful cheer,
While kiwis whisper, "Life's unclear!"

Cucumbers play in salty seas,
Peppers dance upon the breeze.
Each fruit here has a silly way,
To make you smile, come what may.

So take a slice of fruity fun,
Life's a game until we're done.
With every bite, let laughter rise,
In this fruity feast, oh what a prize!

Juices of Time

When time spins like a silky spin,
A blender whirls, let fun begin.
Pineapple yells, "I'm sweet and bold!"
Tomatoes blush, "Stories untold!"

Citrus splash with tangy flair,
While veggie puns fill up the air.
Kiwis joke, "I'm fuzzy inside!"
As watermelons take a ride.

Time drips down in colorful streams,
Lemonade laughter fuels our dreams.
Juices squirt, each drop a jest,
In this blend, we find our best.

So raise your cup, let's cheers today,
With fruity giggles on display.
In every sip, a tale we find,
Juices of time, oh so kind!

Ripe Reflections

In the orchard where fruits collide,
Each one holds a twisty guide.
Plums chuckle, "You missed the point!"
While apples inquire, "Let's anoint!"

Berries bounce off reflective walls,
While melons try to dodge their falls.
Figs are ripe with wisdom to share,
Looking funny, but they don't care.

Peaches whisper, "What's ripe today?"
As nectarines dance in a play.
Lemons roll with a sour pout,
And oranges just laugh it out.

Reflecting smiles with fruity glee,
Isn't life simply peachee?
Each bite a jest, each laugh a gift,
In ripe reflections, spirits lift!

Seeds of Promise

In the garden of hope, seeds do sprout,
Tomatoes giggle, "What's this about?"
Peppers chirp, "We're planting dreams!"
While carrots plot in leafy schemes.

Watermelon wants a sunlit spot,
While strawberries say, "Life's a lot!"
Pumpkins grin, "We'll grow so tall!"
As radishes trickle in for a brawl.

Each seed a promise, full of zest,
Some just want to look their best.
With roots in laughter, all abound,
In the patch of joy, fun is found.

So plant your dreams, and let them rise,
With seeds of promise, reach for the skies.
Each chuckle blooms, as we all grow,
In this garden, humor's the show!

Tasting the Unwritten

In the orchard, smiles abound,
Grapes gossip, making a sound.
Lemons roll with zest and cheer,
Mangoes dance, spreading good cheer.

Peaches blush, they're oh-so shy,
Kiwi winks as the cherries fly.
Pineapple wears a crown so bright,
While plums don capers during the night.

Pears play tricks, hang in a tree,
While tangerines laugh, carefree.
Fruits debate who's the best speller,
As apples jest, "We're the fellers!"

Bananas slip, but what a scene!
Fruitful jokes, ripe for the glean!
Life's a party, come take a bite,
In this happiness, we see the light.

Apricot Affection

Apricots hug in the sun's warm glow,
Tickled by breezes, swaying to and fro.
With hugs so soft, they giggle and grin,
Sharing sweet secrets, laughter within.

Juicy oranges throw a splashy parade,
In citrusy bursts, their antics displayed.
Cherry clowns juggle, oh what a sight,
While figs tell tales through the deep night.

Dates strut in boots, looking so fine,
While apples host parties with fizzy brine.
Overall, it's a fruity affair,
Where laughter and joy fill the air.

Let's make a toast with some juicy punch,
To apricots sweet on a whimsical brunch!
Twirling and twirling, we savor this cheer,
In this nutty world, let's dance and not fear.

Soft Orange Embrace

Soft oranges roll with a gentle hug,
Whispering secrets wrapped snug as a bug.
Persimmons twirl in a delicate waltz,
While juicy limes declare, "No faults!"

Cantaloupes giggle, their rinds so bold,
Telling the tales that need to be told.
Every sweet slice brings laughter and fun,
Under the sun, all worries are done.

Apple pies flop like comedic plays,
As honeydew hums through the sweet summer rays.
Fruits congregate, do the funky dance,
Living out loud, embracing life's chance.

So let's share a laugh, sweet and bright,
With every soft bite, life's pure delight!
Forget all your troubles, let's joyfully stare,
At all the sweet fruits, floating in the air.

Berry Literatures

Berries gather for a wild debate,
Strawberries argue who's truly first-rate.
Raspberries boast of their tart little bite,
While blueberries claim they shine in the night.

Blackberries whisper, "We're misfits, you know,"
"I'm prickly, but charming!" says the one in tow.
Together they weave stories so grand,
In a fruit-filled library, laughter unplanned.

Books made of grapes, so juicy and round,
In this tasty tale, new wonders are found.
Fruits pen their stories under the sun,
Spin tales of sweetness, and endless fun.

So come take a seat, grab a slice of pie,
In this berry kingdom, let the laughter fly!
For every ripe moment, so juicy, sincere,
Tells tales of delight, in life's vibrant sphere.

Orchard Whispers

In an orchard of giggles, apples roll,
They tickle your toes, that's their goal.
Pears wear hats, oh what a sight,
Laughing together, all day and night.

The plums play tag with skittish bees,
While cherries dance in the playful breeze.
Bananas slip by, with a wink and a grin,
In this fruity world, no one feels thin.

Grapes gossip loudly, telling sweet tales,
Of mischievous squirrels and their funny trails.
Each bite a chuckle, each sip a cheer,
In this garden of laughter, joy is near.

With every harvest, a giggle falls,
In this juicy realm, the laughter calls.
So skip through the rows, and join in the fun,
For life's a feast, for everyone.

Cherries on the Path

Cherries are bouncing along the ground,
Rolling and tumbling, what fun can be found!
One pops right up, says, 'Catch me if you can!'
With a wink and a spin, it outsmarts the plan!

Berries are chuckling, sharing sweet pie,
While grapes limp up, with a drunken sigh.
'Are we ripe enough yet?' they giggle in glee,
'Let's wine about it, just you and me!'

Peaches in sunhats, lounging by the stream,
Sipping on nectar with whipped cream dream.
They throw a splash, oh what a blast,
In this wild orchard, a party's amassed!

So join the parade down the fruity lane,
With laughter and joy, it's hard to complain.
Cherries keep rolling, fresh fun never stops,
In this raucous harvest, joy overflows and hops!

Citrus Symphony

Lemons sing high notes, oranges hum low,
Together they create quite the citrus show.
Limes twist in rhythm, dancing with zest,
Citrus cabaret, you know it's the best!

The tangy tunes jive with tropical beats,
With each little bob, the flavor repeats.
Grapefruits tap dance, so round and so bold,
In this fruity fiesta, laughter's controlled.

'Pineapple! Come join!' shouts a flamboyant zest,
'In this fruit orchestra, we're all on our quest!'
Mangoes shake maracas, fruity and grand,
While berries groove to the beat of the band.

So peel away worries, let laughter abound,
In this zesty circus, joy's always found.
Each morsel's a giggle, so sweet and so bright,
In the citrus concert, everything feels right!

Melon Memories

Watermelons tell tales of sun and of fun,
Under the shade, where laughter has spun.
Cantaloupes chuckle, with seeds all around,
Sharing sweet memories and giggles abound.

'Remember that summer?' one melon recalls,
'When we slipped down the hill and broke through the walls?'
They burst into laughter, seeds flinging wide,
In this whimsical world, joy cannot hide.

Honeydews join in with cool, sweet grins,
As fruit salad dreams stir where friendship begins.
With spoons in their hands, they dig in with glee,
Creating a mess, what a sight to see!

So savor the moments, in laughter make haste,
For life's better lived when you fruitfully tasted.
Each slice a delight, each smile a cheer,
In the melon's embrace, joy's always near!

Garden of Hope

In a garden where dreams grow tall,
Tomatoes flirt and the cucumbers call.
Carrots hide under the soil's thick sheet,
While peas pop out to dance on their feet.

Bees buzzing like they're in a race,
Pollinate gossip at a dizzying pace.
Lettuce winks with a leafy green grin,
Saying, "Come sit, let the fun begin!"

Rabbits plotting their veggie heist,
While squirrels debate who's got the best bite.
A whiff of mint makes the chaos swell,
In this garden, there's laughter to tell.

Hope sprouts higher, the sun shines bright,
With every harvest, there's sheer delight.
So grab a fork and join the parade,
In the garden of giggles, all worries fade.

Visions in the Vineyard

In a vineyard of whimsy, grapes hang low,
Chardonnay giggles while Merlot steals the show.
Cabernet whispers, 'We're here for a feast!'
But they all just want to join the grape-eating beast!

Barrels roll like barrels of fun,
While sommeliers dance as they sip on the sun.
From fermented folly to wine-tasting flair,
It's a grape expectation; there's plenty to share.

A cork pops off with a fizzy cheer,
And the grapes all join in the waltz without fear.
Pour out the laughter, let it flow and fill,
In this vineyard of joy, there's always a thrill.

Visions are blurry, the laughter just right,
Under the stars, they'll toast through the night.
So raise your glass and let spirits soar,
For in this grape world, there's always more.

Grapes of Gratitude

In a basket of laughter, grapes sit around,
Joking with apples, 'We're the best in town!'
Strawberries blush, trying to keep up,
While bananas slip with a giggle and a hiccup.

Thankfulness bubbles in each juicy bite,
Sweet fruits gather to share their delight.
They toast to the sunshine, the rain, and the glee,
With every good harvest, they party with tea.

Mangoes and figs are the stars of the show,
Declaring, 'You haven't seen moves like ours flow!'
Pineapples crown themselves kings of the fruit,
While they waltz through the harvest, bold and astute.

Gratitude grows in this fruity parade,
As laughter and joy dance unafraid.
So bite into sweetness, let the fun start,
In the garden of gratitude, love's always part.

Summertime Skies on a Plate

On a plate dressed up with colors so bright,
Summer's sweet bounty is a glorious sight.
Watermelon winks under the sun's warm glow,
While blueberries rally for a juicy show.

Cucumbers dive into a citrusy sea,
Tomatoes gossip, 'Can you believe the spree?'
Lettuce flips cartwheels, all crisp and anew,
While radishes blush in their rosy debut.

The salad bowl's filled with a fruity swirl,
Mangoes are twirling, giving it a whirl.
Each bite's a festival, a sunny delight,
Summertime smiles in every bite, so bright.

With laughs served fresh and the dressing so light,
We savor the season from morning till night.
So dig in, dear friend, let the good times unfold,
On this plate of joy, let the stories be told.

Feasting on Change

Life's buffet is quite a spread,
With mashed potatoes and hopes to shed.
Sometimes sweet, sometimes sour,
It varies by the hour.

Grab a slice of mystery pie,
Whether it's sweet, or makes you cry.
Never fear the odd surprise,
Lemon zest may just arise!

A salad tossed with dreams unfurled,
Tossed with ranch from a crazy world.
So take a scoop of what's to come,
Who knew life was so much fun?

With chocolate drizzle, not so neat,
We laugh and dance while we eat.
Each bite's a chuckle, a tasty punch,
Join the feast, and munch, munch, munch!

Sketches of an Apple

An apple a day, they say with cheer,
But why is it always so near?
Sketches of red, green, and gold,
Stories of fun waiting to be told.

A silly grin, a worm might peek,
In the art of juice, they're oh-so-bleak.
Yet with each crunch, there's laughter loud,
Who knew fruit could make a crowd?

Jokes made of seeds that tend to sprout,
"What's your favorite?" we often shout.
Paintings of cider in every sip,
Raise a toast, let the laughter rip!

In the orchard, clues start to flit,
Every tree has a humorous bit.
So draw and doodle, take a chance,
In this fruity world, we all can dance!

Cane of Sugar

Oh, sugar cane, so tall and proud,
With dreams of sweets that form a crowd.
Twisting and twirling in the sun,
A stick of joy, oh what fun!

From syrupy rivers to candy bars,
You sweeten our lives, like shining stars.
Add a dash of spice, or a giggle too,
Life's a candy shop, and you're the glue!

Lollipops laughing, and chocolates tease,
With every bite, it's purest ease.
They say too much will make you bounce,
But who could resist a merry pounce?

So let's all dance in a sugary daze,
With smiles so bright, and silly ways.
Take a bite, let's sway and swing,
In the candy land where we can sing!

Root of Reflection

Digging down to where smiles grow,
Roots entangled, what a show!
Whispers of laughter in the dirt,
Where every thump can also hurt.

From carrots with quirks to beets with style,
Veggies that giggle and make you smile.
What's this root, so funny and wise?
With leafy hats, they look so spry!

Turning soil into stories grand,
These underground folks will take a stand.
Beneath the surface, the fun begins,
In this garden where laughter wins.

So let's cultivate joy with every sprout,
Watering dreams without a doubt.
As we dig deeper, find your own cheer,
In the roots of life, it's all right here!

Tasting the Colors of Life

A palette of flavors, bright and bold,
Each hue a tale of adventures told.
Bite into rainbows, sweet and tangy,
Life's a party, never too fanny!

Carrots in orange, so crisp, so clear,
They tell funny stories, bring us near.
Blueberries giggle, plump and round,
With each little pop, laughter's found.

Lemons are sour, but hey, that's good,
They add the zing like every food should.
Taste the green, and bring a grin,
In this colorful feast, let joy begin!

So dip and dive into flavors bright,
Each bite's a chuckle, a burst of light.
Life's delicious in every way,
Join the tasting party, come what may!

The Pear's Paradox

A pear once pondered on its shine,
It thought itself more sweet than wine.
But in the fridge, it faced the plight,
Of wedging tight, while others took flight.

A grumpy apple rolled on by,
"Too ripe for pie!" it did cry.
While bananas giggled in their bunch,
"We'll slip and slide; you're just a hunch!"

Cucumber Reflections

In the garden, a cucumber sighed,
"Why am I green? It's not that tried!"
Yet every salad sang its praise,
As it danced in bowls, losing the maze.

A tomato blushed, feeling quite hot,
"We're in this salad, like it or not!"
In a vinaigrette, they'd weave and twine,
Making a dish that's perfectly fine.

Cherries of Change

Two cherries on a tree so grand,
Argued about the band they'd stand.
"Let's sing a tune!" said one with flair,
The other just giggled, with no care.

Together they swayed in sun-soaked cheer,
Plucking up laughter, year after year.
A sprinkle of juice, they laughed at fate,
"Life's a pit stop; let's roller skate!"

Satin of the Citrus

An orange wore a silky sheen,
Touting its zest, it felt like a queen.
Lemons stood by, pouting in green,
"Why do you shine? We're all on the scene!"

But the lime chimed in with a twist and a shout,
"Let's mix it up; that's what it's about!"
In cocktails or solo, each fruit held tight,
In the raucous dance of a fruity delight!

Pears and Possibilities

Pears ripened on the tree,
Joking in the breeze,
"What if we ran away?"
Said one to another, "What a tease!"

Juicy laughter fills the air,
As bees do waltz and twirl,
Each bite a step, a daring dare,
Chasing dreams in fruity swirl.

In a bowl we sit and scheme,
Wondering who will take the lead,
"Let's mix with apples in their dream!"
Fruit punch frolic, oh yes, indeed!

So pack your bags, let's make a plan,
To roll and tumble down the street,
Life's a juicy, merry can,
Together we shall dance and eat!

Pomegranate Parables

In a garden bright and fair,
A pomegranate told a joke,
"I'm full of seeds, but do I care?"
His laughter burst, oh what a yoke!

Each ruby drop, a story spun,
Of silly days in sundry hues,
"Join me for some pun, just one!"
They blushed in purple, making news.

"Let's make a mess!" the others cried,
"Let's splash our juice on every wall!"
Together giggling side by side,
A fruity party, what a ball!

So heed this tale of zest and fun,
Find joy in every little pith,
In every burst, your laugh will run,
And life, my friend, becomes a myth!

Grapes of Growth

Grapes in a bunch, so full of glee,
Swaying like dancers on a vine,
"We're all in this together, you see!"
A hiccup here, a cheer divine!

From green to purple, we take a ride,
Each one waiting for summer's call,
Sliding down like a roller slide,
Round and round, we never fall!

In the evening sun, we hold a feast,
With laughter ringing in the air,
"Let's toast to fun! Our joy increased!"
Grapes giggle without a care.

So raise a glass, let's splash some cheer,
Within this bunch, we're all the same,
Life's grape fun is always near,
Just roll with it, no need for blame!

Fragments of Flavor

In a bowl of color, a zesty spread,
A citrus twist with a wacky grin,
"What's life without flavor?" they said,
Each fragment a wish in every spin!

Fruits of all kinds mix and mingle,
Bananas dip and cherries bounce,
"Let's start a band! We'll make hearts tingle!"
With fruity beats, they all pronounce.

Tangerines twirl, while kiwis call,
"Join our jam, it's sticky sweet!"
With every slice, we're having a ball,
Flavorful dreams in every beat!

So here's to the mix, the laughter loud,
In the salad of life, we're the zest,
Stick with the fun, be fruity and proud,
In this vibrant dance, we are blessed!

Tapestry of Tastes

In a bowl of quirky dreams,
Bananas dance, or so it seems.
Grapes in tiny, purple huddles,
Laugh at life and all its cuddles.

Pineapples wear their crowns so proud,
While lemons scowl, so very loud.
A cherry giggles with delight,
As oranges roll away from fright.

Peaches blush, their rumors fly,
Strawberries sing sweet lullabies.
Kiwi's antics keep it neat,
As pears shuffle on tiny feet.

Oh, the flavor on this stage,
Each one plays out its own age.
Mixing laughter, joy, and cheer,
In a feast that's oh-so-dear!

Blossoms of Tomorrow

Budded blooms of zesty charms,
Petal whispers, sweet and warms.
Daisies snicker in the sun,
While tulips play a prank for fun.

Sunflower jokes are tall and bright,
Their silly faces in pure light.
Daffodils with giggles burst,
In a flowery bubble, they're conversed.

Lilies wave with gentle grace,
Trying hard to win the race.
Forget-me-nots, they just won't quit,
Their heartfelt wishes often flit.

Gardens filled with grins galore,
Every bloom opens a door.
Laughter blossoms without cease,
In this world of floral peace!

Nectar of Nostalgia

Sip that honeyed, syrupy blend,
Memories of days that never end.
Sticky traces on your chin,
A giggle here, and a playful spin.

Old jam jars stacked upon a shelf,
Reflect the love of our sweet self.
Cottage gatherings, spills abound,
Every bite brings joy profound.

Grandma's pie, a cherished laugh,
Flavors blend—a lovely craft.
Days of sunshine, skips, and hops,
Where sweet silliness never stops.

A spoon of joy, a dash of cheer,
Spreading smiles year after year.
In every taste, a tale unfolds,
Of times we cherished, forever gold!

Juicy Revelations

A pulpy truth spills from this rhyme,
Fruits of wisdom share their time.
Dates confess their past romances,
While ripe figs lead rom-com dances.

A watermelon's laughter flows,
Splashing seeds where the sunshine glows.
Lemons squawk with zesty zest,
In the juicy world, they jest.

Raspberry whispers tales of fun,
How blue skies blend with everyone.
Tart moments round, yet oh-so sweet,
In every slice, a fun retreat.

So take a bite, don't hesitate,
In each fruit, a chance to celebrate.
Savor joy, let laughter soar,
In this juicy land, there's always more!

www.ingramcontent.com/pod-product-compliance
Lightning Source LLC
Chambersburg PA
CBHW070304120526
44590CB00017B/2561